HOW MY BODY **WORKS**

Blood

Anita Ganeri

Evans Brothers Limited

First published by Evans Brothers Limited in 2006
2a Portman Mansions
Chiltern St
London W1U 6NR

British Library Cataloguing in Publication Data
Ganeri, Anita
Blood Red
        1. Blood - Circulation - Juvenile literature
        2. Human physiology - Juvenile literature
        I. Title

ISBN 0 237 53186 0
13-digit ISBN (from 1 January 2007) 978 0 237 53186 7

Credits
Editorial: Louise John
Design: Mark Holt & Big Blu Design
Artworks: Julian Baker
Consultant: Dr M Turner
Photographs: Steve Shott
Production: Jenny Mulvanny

Printed in China by WKT Co. Ltd

Acknowledgements
The author and publisher would like to thank the following
for kind permission to reproduce photographs:

Science Photo Library, p.11 (National Cancer Institute),
p.12 (Professors PM Motta and S Correr), p.15 (Alfred
Pasieka), p.17 (Damien Lovegrove), p.27 (left), p.27 (right);
Bruce Coleman Collection, p.23.

Models from the Norrie Carr Agency and Truly
Scrumptious Ltd. With thanks to: Sara Velmi, Max Wybourn,
Jake Clark, Mia Powell, Lauren Chapple, Courtney Thomas,
Bethan Matthews and Skye Johnson and also Ellen and Jack
Millard. Copyright © Evans Brothers Ltd 2003.

VISIT OUR WEBSITE
Evans
www.evansbooks.co.uk

Contents

Blood-red blood

A very special liquid is flowing through your whole body. What is it? Blood-red blood, of course. It's the red, sticky stuff that seeps out of you if you cut yourself. Your blood has important jobs to do. It carries useful things, such as **oxygen** from the air you breathe, and goodness from the food you eat, to every part of you. It collects waste, such as **carbon dioxide** gas, so you can get rid of it. Your useful blood also helps your body to fight off harmful **germs**.

LOOK AT ME! ◉ LOOK AT ME! ◉ LOOK AT ME! ◉ LOOK AT ME! ◉ LOOK AT ME!

When you were born, you had less than a litre of blood in your body – about two mugfuls. Adults have about five litres of blood – about half a bucketful.

Your blood does not simply flow through you. It is pushed along by a strong muscle in your chest, called your heart. Every time your amazing heart beats, it squeezes blood around your body, through lots of tiny tubes. Your heart has to keep beating, day and night, to keep your blood flowing.

AMAZING!

Your heart and blood are called your circulatory system. You can see the different parts in the picture. "Circulatory" means going round and round.

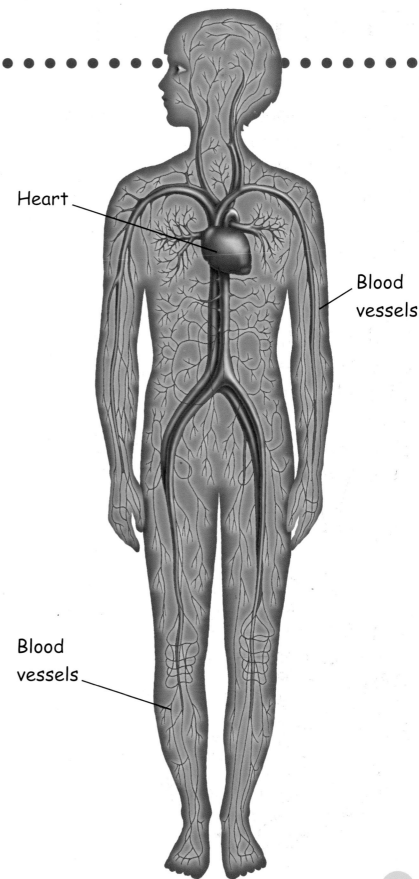

Heart

Blood vessels

Blood vessels

9

What is blood?

Your blood is a red, sticky liquid that flows around you, all the time. More than half of your blood is made from a watery fluid, called plasma. But if you looked at a drop of blood under a **microscope**, you'd see that plasma has lots of tiny bits floating about in it. These are your blood **cells**. Your blood cells are made inside some of the large bones in your body.

LOOK AT ME! LOOK AT ME! LOOK AT ME! LOOK AT ME! LOOK AT ME!

Dissolve some sugar in a jar of warm water. Add two teaspoons of tea leaves and give it a shake. This is what blood cells look like floating in plasma.

TEA

Red blood cells pick up oxygen when your blood passes through your lungs. They carry it around your body. White blood cells gobble up germs and help your body to fight illnesses. Platelets are tiny bits of cells, floating in the plasma. They help to stop you bleeding when you cut yourself.

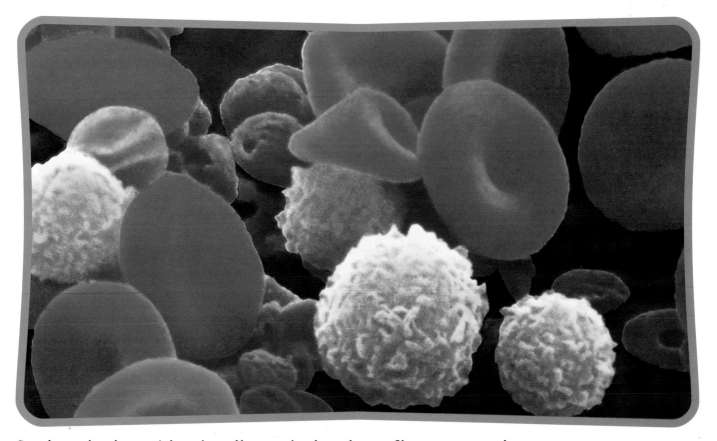

Red and white blood cells and platelets floating in plasma, seen under a microscope.

Why is blood red?

Your red blood cells are tiny but you have lots of them – about 30 billion billion in all. That's more than any other type of cell in your whole body. They are shaped a bit like doughnuts, with a dip in the middle.

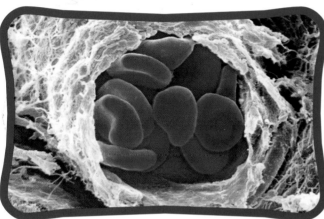

Red blood cells, seen through a microscope.

AMAZING!

Red blood cells live for about four months. Then your body makes new ones. In this time, they travel around your body more than 150,000 times.

Your red blood cells have a special chemical in them. It is called **haemoglobin** (heem-ow-glow-bin). In your lungs, oxygen from the air you breathe sticks to the haemoglobin. This turns your blood bright red. Then your blood carries the oxygen all around your body. Your body needs oxygen to make it work. The oxygen mixes with the food you eat to give you energy. When the oxygen is used up, your stale blood turns purply-blue.

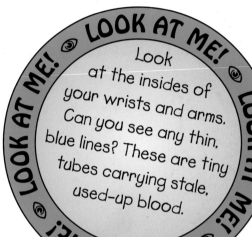

LOOK AT ME! Look at the insides of your wrists and arms. Can you see any thin, blue lines? These are tiny tubes carrying stale, used-up blood.

White blood cells

Your white blood cells look white under a microscope but they are not really white. They are made from a see-through stuff, like clear jelly. White blood cells are bigger than red blood cells. They help your body to destroy the harmful germs that can cause illnesses.

LOOK AT ME! LOOK AT ME! LOOK AT ME! LOOK AT ME!

Taking your temperature tells you if you have a fever. If you are ill your body needs a good rest so it can fight against germs.

14

Germs get into your body through your nose and mouth, or through cuts and grazes. Inside you, they grow and attack your cells, making you ill. As your body starts to fight back, you might get symptoms, such as a fever, aches and pains or feeling sick.

Some white blood cells surround germs and gobble them up whole. Other white blood cells make **chemicals**, which stick on to germs and kill them. These cells make thousands of different kinds of chemicals to protect your body against different sorts of germs.

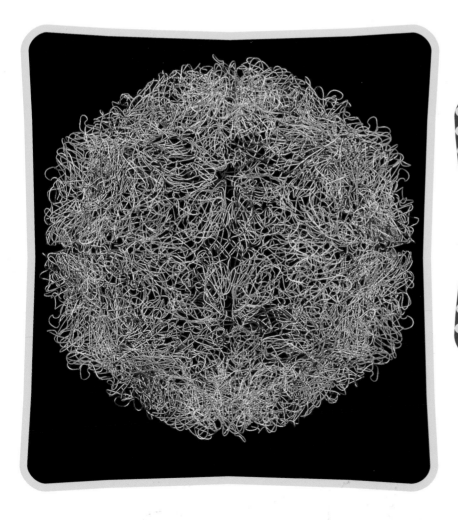

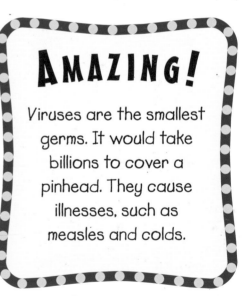

AMAZING!

Viruses are the smallest germs. It would take billions to cover a pinhead. They cause illnesses, such as measles and colds.

This is the virus that causes colds.

Plasma and platelets

About half of your blood is a pale, yellowish liquid called plasma. Your blood cells float in it. Plasma is mostly water but it also carries goodness from the food you eat. Your body uses this goodness to grow, mend worn-out parts and to give you energy. The plasma also carries waste away.

LOOK AT ME! LOOK AT ME! LOOK AT ME! LOOK AT ME!

Sometimes you need a sticking plaster to keep a wound clean and help it to heal.

Platelets are tiny cells, even smaller than your red blood cells. Platelets help your blood to clot when you cut yourself. This stops you from bleeding too much. The platelets make a tough, hard scab to protect the wound while your skin is healing.

Some people give their blood to help others who are ill or injured and need new blood.

There are four different groups of blood. They are called A, B, O and AB. Your blood group depends on special chemicals in your red blood cells and your plasma. Doctors can do tests to find out which blood group you belong to.

AMAZING!

Ill people may need a **blood transfusion** to help them get better. But they must be given blood from a matching group to their own.

Blood vessels

Your blood flows around your body through thin tubes, called blood vessels. **Arteries** are blood vessels that carry blood from your heart around your body. They have thick walls to stop blood from leaking out. The walls are stretchy so they do not break with the force of the flowing blood.

LOOK AT ME! Look in the mirror and gently pull your lower eyelid down. Can you see some red thready bits? These are some of the tiniest blood vessels in your body.

The blood vessels branch out and get smaller, until they are too tiny to see. They are now called **capillaries**. They reach every part of your body. Capillaries have very thin walls so that oxygen and goodness from your food can seep out of your blood and into your body.

Your capillaries join up again to make thicker tubes, called **veins**. They carry blood back to your heart. In your veins, there are tiny flaps, called valves. They stop your blood from flowing backwards.

AMAZING!

If you put all your blood vessels end to end, they would stretch twice around the world!

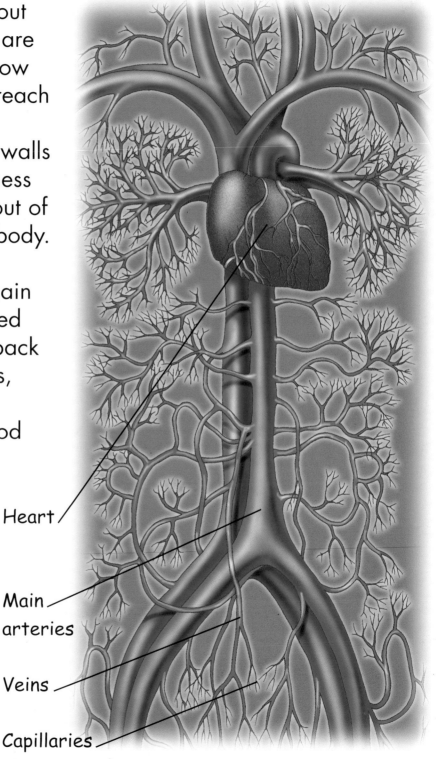

Heart

Main arteries

Veins

Capillaries

Have a heart

Your heart sits in the middle of your chest, slightly to the left, between your two lungs. Its job is to pump blood around your body, day and night. This lets your blood carry oxygen and goodness from your food to all the parts of your body.

LOOK AT ME! LOOK AT ME! LOOK AT ME! LOOK AT ME!

Clench your fist tightly. Now it's about the same size as your amazing heart.

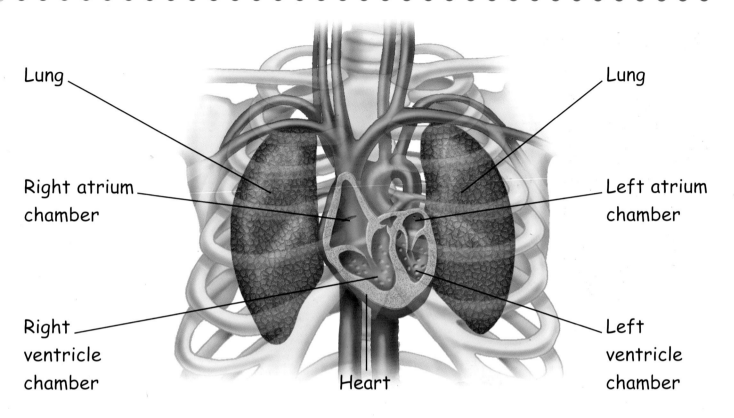

Lung

Right atrium chamber

Right ventricle chamber

Lung

Left atrium chamber

Left ventricle chamber

Heart

Your heart is a special muscle. Unlike the muscles in your arms and legs, your heart never gets tired. It keeps on working throughout your life, all the time. The muscles in your heart work a bit like a bicycle pump. They squeeze to push the blood out and around your body.

Your heart is divided into four parts, called chambers. They have strong muscle walls in between them. Thick flaps called valves connect the top two chambers with the two chambers below.

AMAZING!

Your heart grows bigger as you do. An adult's heart weighs about the same as a large potato!

Heart beat

Each pump of your heart is called a heartbeat. Each time your heart beats, stale blood from your body flows into the right side of your heart. Then it is pumped into your lungs to collect fresh supplies of oxygen. Then blood from your lungs flows into the left side of your heart. Your heart squeezes and pumps it all around your body, through your blood vessels.

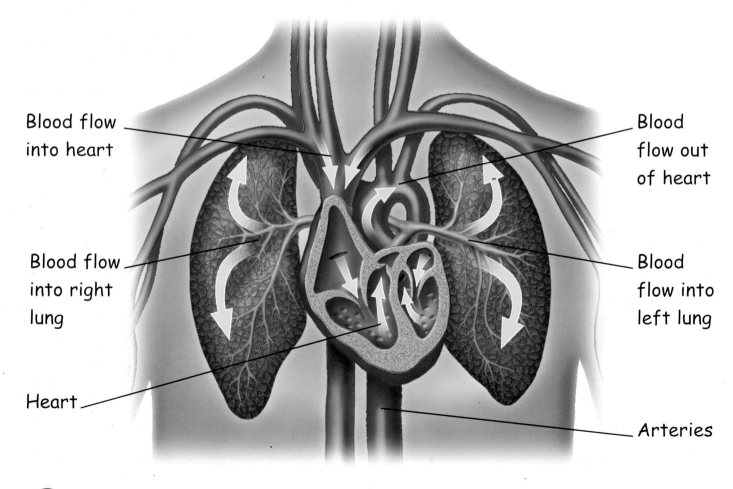

Blood flow into heart

Blood flow into right lung

Heart

Blood flow out of heart

Blood flow into left lung

Arteries

An elephant's heart beats very slowly.

Special flaps in your heart, called valves, open to let blood flow through. Then they snap shut to stop the blood flowing backwards again. This makes the "thump thump" sound you can hear as a heartbeat. Doctors use instruments called stethoscopes to listen to people's hearts. The stethoscope makes the heartbeat easier to hear.

AMAZING!

An elephant's heart beats about 25 times a minute. A shrew's heart beats an amazing 600 times.

Fast and slow

Your heart needs to beat all the time. Otherwise your body would die. But you do not need to think about it. It happens automatically. Your amazing heart beats about 80 times a minute. That's more than 100,000 times a day. Each time your heart beats, blood spurts out of it and around your body. You can feel this spurt throbbing in your wrist or in your neck. This is called your **pulse**.

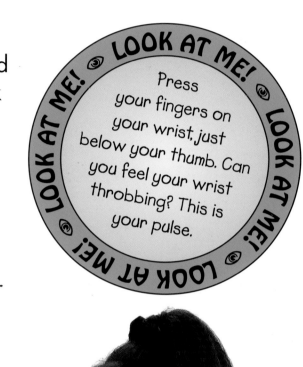

LOOK AT ME! LOOK AT ME! LOOK AT ME! LOOK AT ME!

Press your fingers on your wrist, just below your thumb. Can you feel your wrist throbbing? This is your pulse.

The number of times your heart beats depends on what you are doing. It beats faster when you are doing exercise. This is because your heart needs to pump more blood around your body as your body needs more food and oxygen to keep it going. When you're asleep, your body needs less food and oxygen. So your heart beats more slowly.

LOOK AT ME! LOOK AT ME! LOOK AT ME! LOOK AT ME!

If you put your hand on your chest when you've been running, you can feel your heart beating quite fast.

Healthy heart

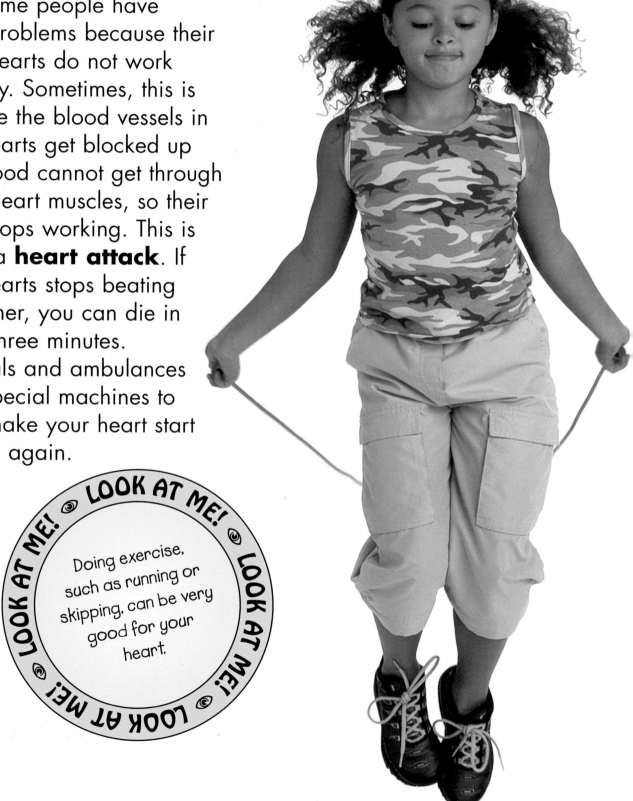

Some people have problems because their hearts do not work properly. Sometimes, this is because the blood vessels in their hearts get blocked up and blood cannot get through to the heart muscles, so their heart stops working. This is called a **heart attack**. If your hearts stops beating altogether, you can die in about three minutes. Hospitals and ambulances have special machines to try to make your heart start beating again.

LOOK AT ME! LOOK AT ME! LOOK AT ME! LOOK AT ME! LOOK AT ME!

Doing exercise, such as running or skipping, can be very good for your heart.

Some people are born with weak hearts. They may need an operation to make them better. People who smoke cigarettes, eat too much or are overweight can also do damage to their hearts. The best way to look after your heart is to eat healthy food and do regular exercise. Then your amazing heart will stay fit and strong for many years to come.

AMAZING!

Today, doctors can do an operation called a heart transplant. They take the old heart out and put a new one in.

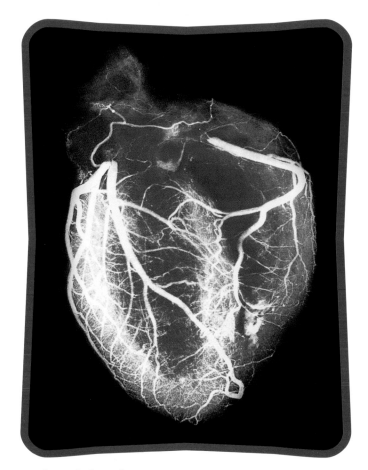

A healthy heart.

A heart with blocked blood vessels.

Glossary

Arteries The blood vessels which carry blood from your heart to your body.

Blood transfusion When a person's blood is exchanged for a fresh blood supply.

Blood vessels The thin tubes which carry blood around your body.

Capillaries The tiniest blood vessels in your body.

Carbon dioxide A waste gas made in your body, which you have to breathe out.

Cells The tiny building blocks which make up every part of your body.

Chemicals Substances in your body which do different jobs.

Germs Tiny living things which cause some illnesses.

Haemoglobin A chemical in your blood which carries oxygen. It is what makes your blood look red.

Heart attack When a person's heart stops working because blood is not able to reach it.

Microscope An instrument used to look at objects which are too tiny to see otherwise.

Oxygen A gas from the air which you need to breathe to stay alive.

Pulse The throbbing feeling in your wrist or neck each time your heart beats and sends blood spurting around your body.

Veins The blood vessels which carry blood from your body to your heart.

Index